Grandfather's Words of Wisdom

A KEEPSAKE JOURNAL OF ADVICE, LESSONS, AND LOVE FOR MY GRANDCHILD

Grandfather's Words of Wisdom

A KEEPSAKE JOURNAL OF ADVICE, LESSONS, AND LOVE FOR MY GRANDCHILD

L.L. Buller

Bluestreak
BOOKS

Bluestreak

an imprint of Weldon Owen International
PO Box 3088, San Rafael, CA 94912
www.weldonowen.com

© 2020 Weldon Owen

Library of Congress Cataloging in Publication data is available.

Printed in China

ISBN-13: 978-1-68188-754-8

10 9 8 7 6 5 4 3 2 1

Contents

Introduction

A Private Note to Grandkids

Grandfathers come in many varieties. Some cheer you on as you wobble away on your very first bike ride. Others always have a piece of candy hidden in their pocket just for you. Some throw you the pitch that you hit for miles. Grandfathers may help you with your homework or show you the best way to climb a tree, catch a fish, or toast the perfect marshmallow. Would you like to find out more about your grandfather and all the things he's learned? Share this journal with him. You will probably be in for some surprises, but you will definitely find out much more about this person who's shared such wonderful times with you.

A LETTER TO MY GRANDCHILD(REN), FROM MY HEART TO YOURS

_____

_____

_____

_____

_____

_____

_____

_____

_____

_____

_____

_____

_____

_____

_____

_____

Written on _____

As I write this, I am in _____

_____

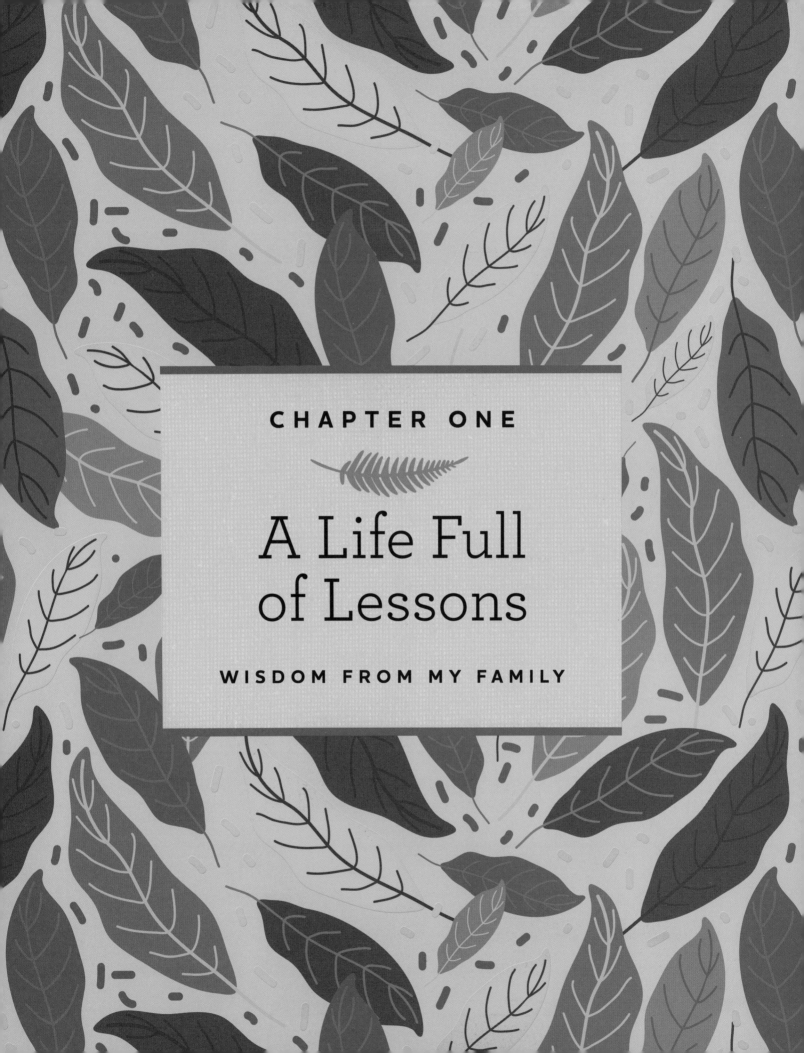

CHAPTER ONE

A Life Full of Lessons

WISDOM FROM MY FAMILY

About Me

Grandpas bring a little wisdom, happiness, warmth, and love to every life they touch.

—UNKNOWN

I was born on _____

_____

I was born in _____

_____

A little bit about my family at the time _____

_____

_____

_____

_____

_____

_____

A special story I want to share about my family _____

_____

_____

_____

_____

_____

_____

_____

_____

_____

_____

_____

_____

_____

_____

_____

_____

_____

_____

_____

Our Family History

I don't know who my grandfather was, I am much more concerned to know what his grandson will be.

—ABRAHAM LINCOLN

Our family names are _____

_____

Our relatives came from _____

_____

_____

Some customs we observed from our heritage were _____

_____

_____

_____

_____

_____

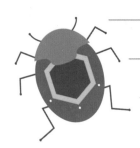

We also shared these religious traditions _____

_____

_____

_____

One life lesson I learned from my relatives is _____

_____

_____

_____

A family saying I've heard all my life is _____

_____

_____

_____

_____

Our family motto could be _____

_____

_____

_____

_____

A Family Foundation

There are only two lasting bequests we can give to
our children—one is roots, and the other, wings.

—HODDING S. CARTER

All in all, my early childhood was _____

_____

_____

_____

_____

I depended on my family for _____

_____

_____

_____

_____

When I needed advice, the relative I turned to was _____

_____

_____

_____

_____

The person who taught me the most was _____

_____

_____

_____

_____

Something my family passed down to me that I'd like you to know _____

_____

_____

_____

I am grateful to my family for teaching me

_____

_____

_____

_____

_____

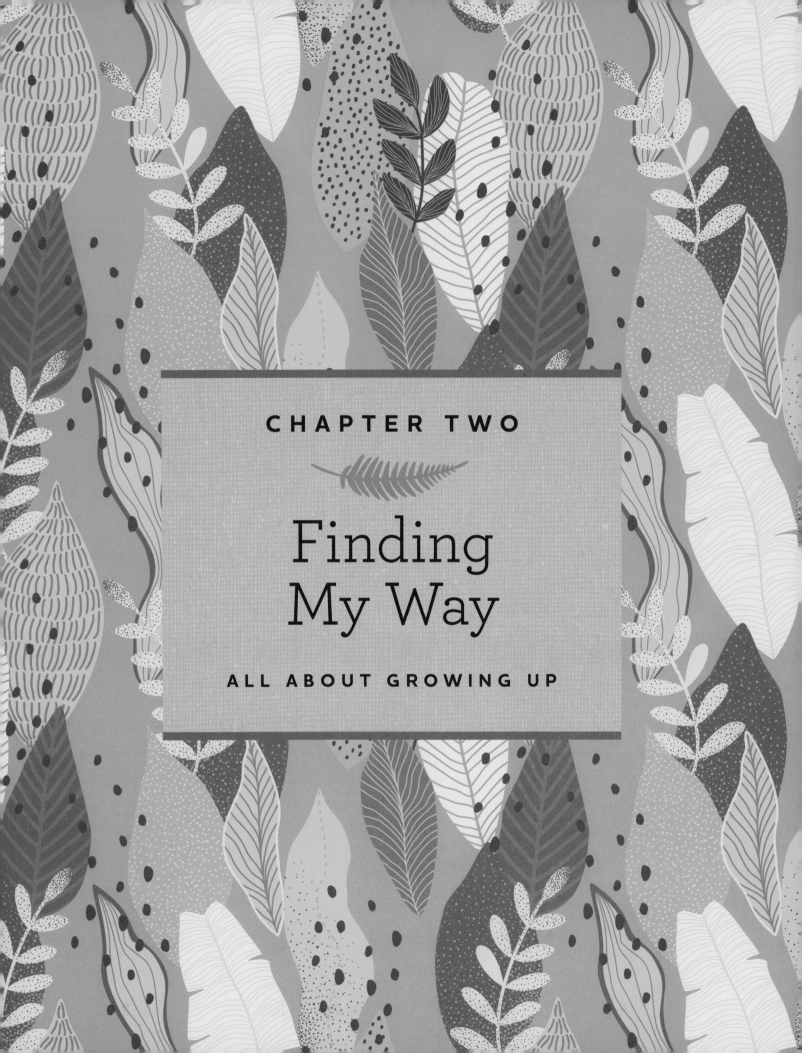

CHAPTER TWO

Finding My Way

ALL ABOUT GROWING UP

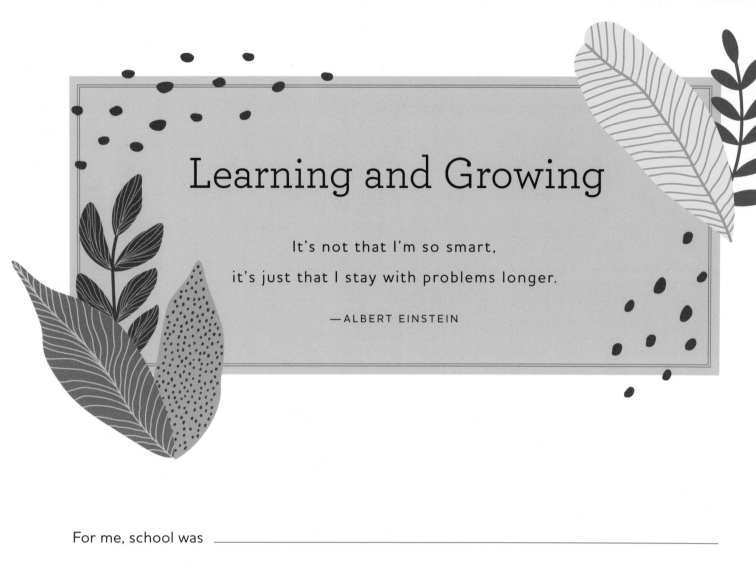

Learning and Growing

It's not that I'm so smart,

it's just that I stay with problems longer.

—ALBERT EINSTEIN

For me, school was _____

_____

_____

_____

_____

_____

_____

My favorite teacher was _____

_____

_____

_____

_____

Some things I learned in class that I still remember are

_____

_____

_____

The important things I learned outside of the classroom were _____

_____

_____

_____

_____

_____

I got through challenges at school by _____

_____

_____

_____

_____

_____

My hopes and dreams for you at school are _____

_____

_____

_____

_____

Making Friends

We need old friends to help us grow old and
new friends to help us stay young.

—LETTY COTTIN POGREBIN

Friendship is so important because _____

_____

_____

_____

_____

_____

My best friends were _____

_____

_____

_____

_____

We loved to _____

_____

_____

_____

_____

_____

A secret we shared together was _____

_____

_____

_____

_____

_____

_____

My advice for making friends is _____

_____

_____

_____

_____

_____

_____

Friendships can be tricky sometimes because

_____

_____

_____

_____

_____

_____

_____

A story about a time a friendship was tested _____

_____

_____

_____

_____

_____

_____

_____

_____

_____

This is what I learned _____

_____

_____

_____

_____

_____

_____

My advice for keeping good friends is _____

_____

_____

_____

_____

_____

I am grateful to my friends because _____

_____

_____

_____

_____

_____

_____

My Family and Me

Other things may change us, but we start
and end with the family.

—ANTHONY BRANDT

As I grew older, my feelings about my family were _____

_____

_____

_____

I became close to _____

_____

_____

_____

_____

My family helped me to learn and grow by _____

_____

_____

_____

_____

_____

One of my favorite memories from that time is _____

_____

_____

_____

_____

_____

_____

The best advice I had from my family was _____

_____

_____

_____

_____

_____

_____

Becoming Me

Be yourself—everyone else is already taken.

—OSCAR WILDE

My teenage years weren't always easy, but I learned _____

_____

_____

_____

_____

_____

I made mistakes sometimes, like _____

_____

_____

_____

_____

My advice to you is _____

_____

_____

_____

_____

_____

I learned to become more myself when _____

_____

_____

_____

_____

_____

One thing to always keep in mind is _____

_____

_____

_____

_____

_____

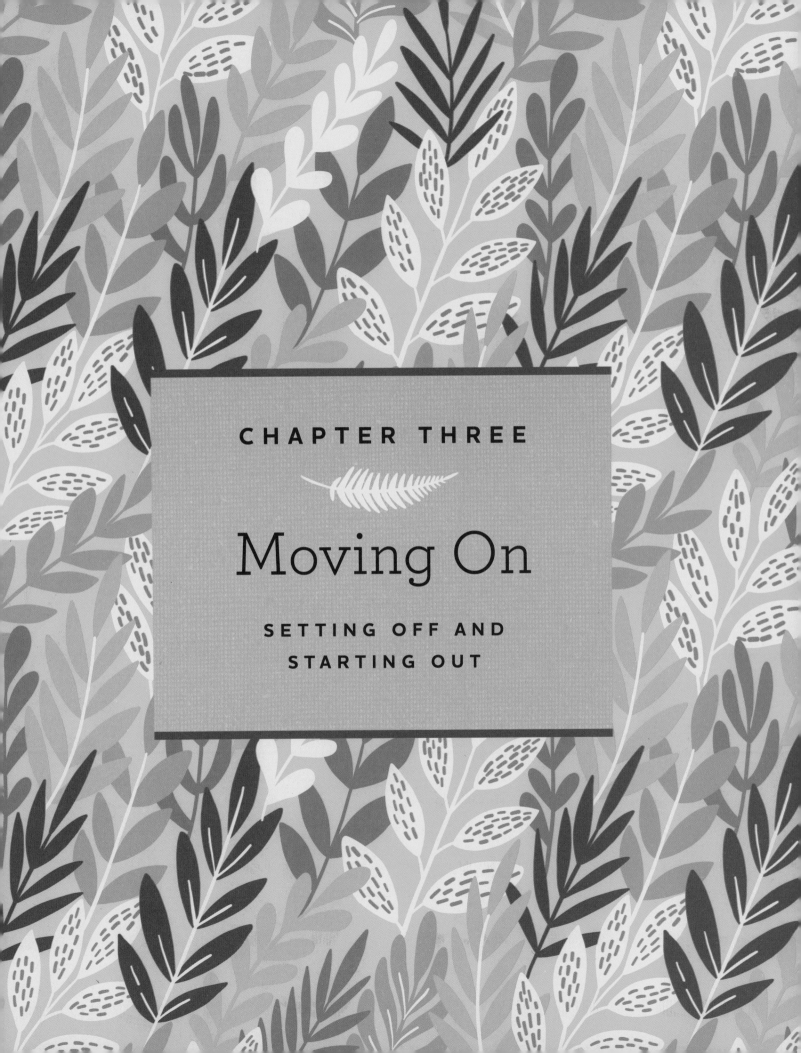

CHAPTER THREE

Moving On

SETTING OFF AND STARTING OUT

Leaving Home

The most lively young people become
the best old people.

—HERMANN HESSE

I was ready to leave the nest when _____

_____

_____

_____

_____

How I felt about leaving home _____

_____

_____

_____

_____

_____

The things I looked forward to were _____

_____

_____

_____

_____

_____

I knew I would be sad about _____

_____

_____

_____

_____

_____

_____

My advice to you when you are thinking of setting off on your own is _____

_____

_____

_____

_____

_____

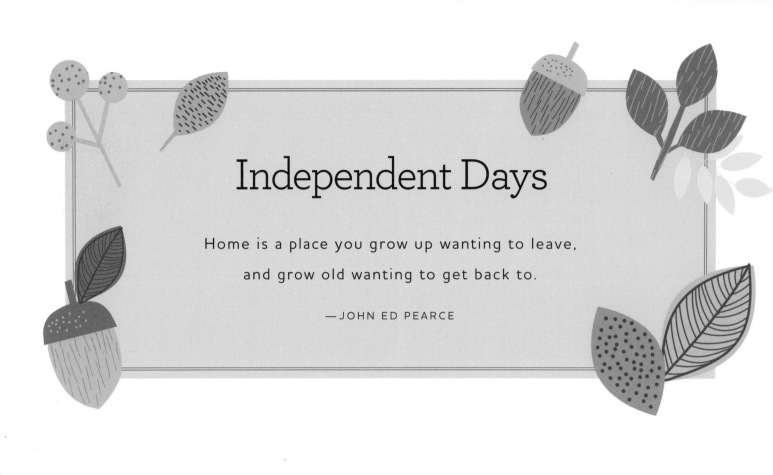

Independent Days

Home is a place you grow up wanting to leave,
and grow old wanting to get back to.

—JOHN ED PEARCE

A story about leaving home for the first time _____

_____

_____

_____

_____

The thing I missed the most was _____

_____

_____

_____

_____

_____

_____

I was most proud of myself for _____

_____

_____

_____

_____

_____

A few mistakes I made were _____

_____

_____

_____

_____

_____

_____

The family advice that I remembered was _____

_____

_____

_____

_____

_____

My brightest dreams for you when you leave home are

_____

_____

_____

_____

_____

_____

_____

_____

_____

_____

_____

_____

_____

_____

_____

_____

_____

_____

My best advice to you for achieving those dreams is _____

_____

_____

_____

_____

_____

_____

_____

_____

_____

_____

_____

_____

_____

_____

_____

_____

_____

How to Be an Adult

I am still every age that I have been. . . . If I can
retain a child's awareness and joy, then I will really
learn what it means to be grown up.

—MADELINE L'ENGLE

I felt grown up for the first time when _____

_____

_____

_____

_____

One thing I know now that I wish I'd known then is _____

_____

_____

_____

_____

I always want you to remember these things about standing on your own two feet

_____

_____

_____

_____

_____

_____

But it's always OK to _____

_____

_____

_____

_____

You know you're doing a great job when _____

_____

_____

_____

_____

_____

_____

Love Is the Answer

Nobody is perfect until you fall in love with them.

—UNKNOWN

Falling in love is so complicated because _____
_____
_____

One thing I'd like you to know about being in love is _____
_____
_____
_____

One thing I'd like you to know about heartbreak is _____
_____
_____
_____

I learned that you know you are in love when _____

_____

_____

_____

_____

A story about love in my own life that I want to share with you _____

_____

_____

_____

_____

_____

_____

_____

_____

_____

_____

_____

_____

_____

My Own Family

You can learn many things from children.
How much patience you have, for instance.

—FRANKLIN P. ADAMS

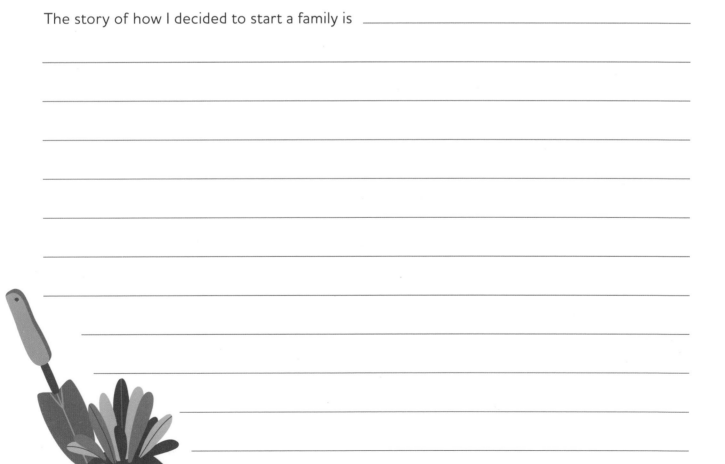

The story of how I decided to start a family is _____

_____

_____

_____

_____

_____

_____

_____

_____

I was excited because _____

_____

_____

_____

_____

I was anxious about _____

_____

_____

_____

_____

_____

_____

The things I wanted to pass down to my children were _____

_____

_____

_____

_____

_____

_____

_____

Being a parent is a huge responsibility. I felt

_____

_____

_____

_____

_____

_____

_____

_____

When your parent was young _____

_____

_____

_____

_____

_____

_____

_____

_____

I knew I was doing a good job when _____

_____

_____

_____

_____

_____

My advice if you decide to start a family of your own is _____

_____

_____

_____

_____

_____

_____

_____

_____

_____

_____

_____

_____

Family Love

In every conceivable manner, the family is a
link to our past, bridge to our future.

—ALEX HALEY

Having children of my own taught me a lot about my own family. I learned

_____

_____

_____

_____

_____

I was grateful to my family for _____

_____

_____

_____

_____

I wish I had known _____

_____

_____

_____

_____

My family relationships changed because _____

_____

_____

_____

_____

_____

_____

A story about seeing my own children with my family members _____

_____

_____

_____

_____

_____

_____

_____

_____

_____

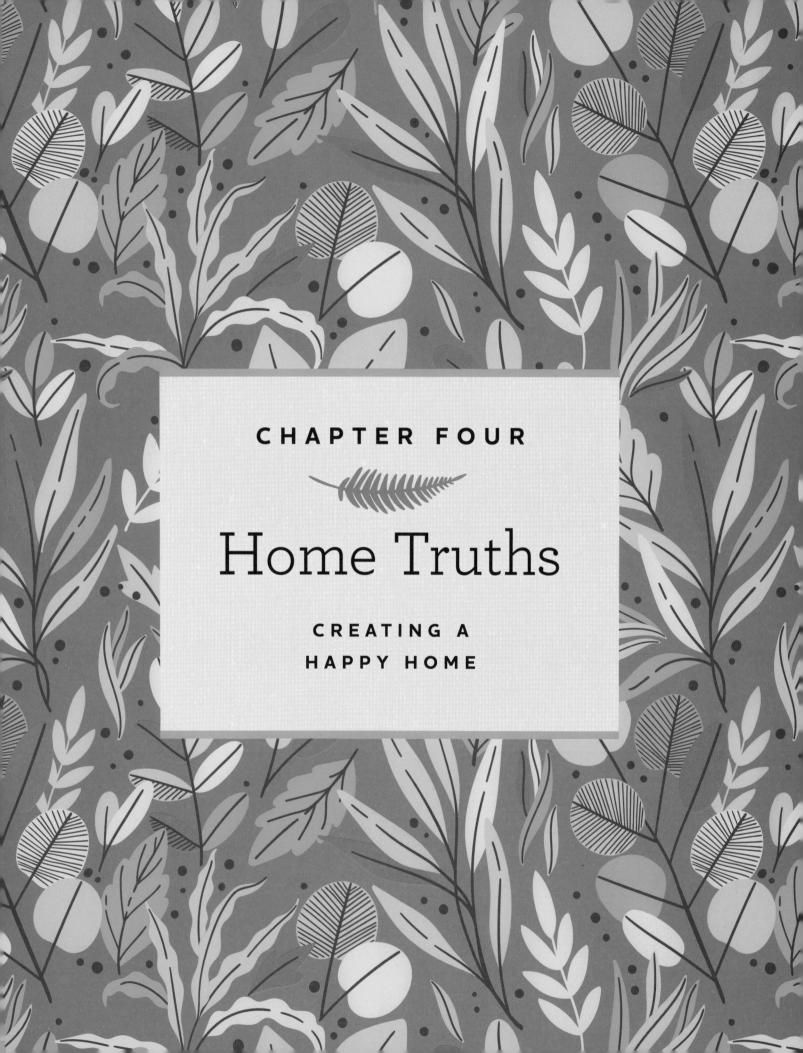

CHAPTER FOUR

Home Truths

CREATING A HAPPY HOME

A Happy Home

Home isn't where you're from, it's where
you find light when all grows dark.

—PIERCE BROWN

Let me tell you a little about our first family home _____

_____

_____

_____

_____

_____

_____

_____

The thing I was proudest of was _____

_____

_____

_____

What made it feel like home was _____

_____

_____

_____

When my family visited I felt _____

_____

_____

_____

I think you need these ingredients for a happy home _____

_____

_____

_____

_____

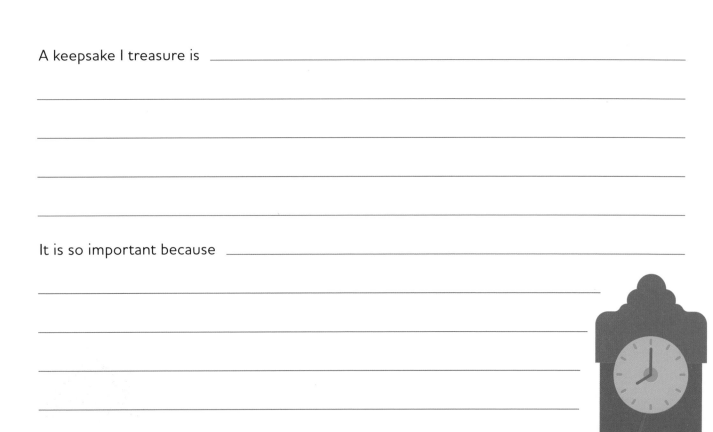

Keepsakes and Memories

The heart, like the mind, has a memory. And in it
are kept the most precious keepsakes.

—HENRY WADSWORTH LONGFELLOW

A keepsake I treasure is _____

_____

_____

_____

_____

It is so important because _____

_____

_____

_____

_____

_____

Something you gave me that brings me happiness is _____

_____

And this is why _____

_____

_____

_____

_____

_____

_____

What objects are worth holding on to _____

_____

_____

_____

_____

When it's okay to let go of something _____

_____

_____

_____

_____

Special Times

A grandfather has the wisdom of long experience
and the love of an understanding heart.

—UNKNOWN

I looked forward to your visits because

_____

_____

_____

_____

Your favorite stories to hear were _____

_____

_____

_____

_____

_____

Your nickname for me was _____

_____

_____

_____

_____

The songs we loved to sing were _____

_____

_____

_____

_____

Something that always made you giggle was _____

_____

_____

_____

_____

The best game we played together was _____

_____

_____

_____

_____

Something I taught you how to do was _____

_____

_____

_____

_____

_____

_____

_____

_____

Something you taught me how to do was _____

_____

_____

_____

_____

_____

_____

_____

The places I remember exploring with you were _____

_____

_____

_____

_____

_____

_____

I could see a little of myself in you when _____

_____

_____

_____

_____

_____

From our times together, I learned _____

_____

_____

_____

_____

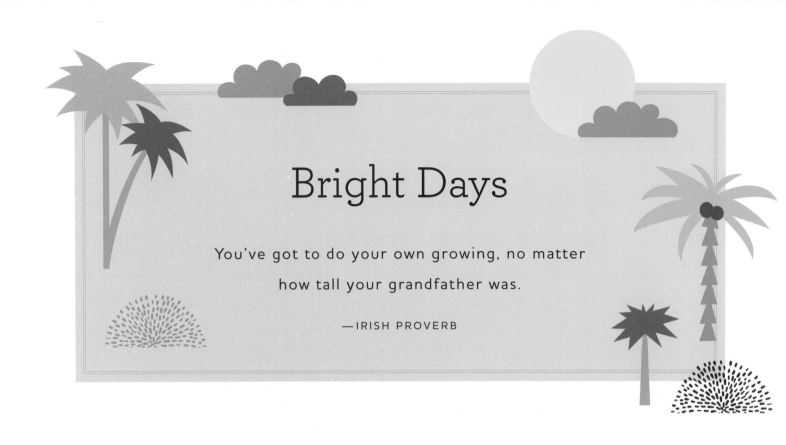

Bright Days

You've got to do your own growing, no matter
how tall your grandfather was.

—IRISH PROVERB

Little things can make your home a happy one. For example, _____

_____

_____

_____

_____

_____

_____

_____

_____

_____

Take a little time every day to feel thankful for your family. Here's how:

_____

_____

_____

_____

_____

_____

Helping other people can make you happy. Why not _____

_____

_____

_____

_____

_____

In my life, these small things have always brought me joy _____

_____

_____

_____

_____

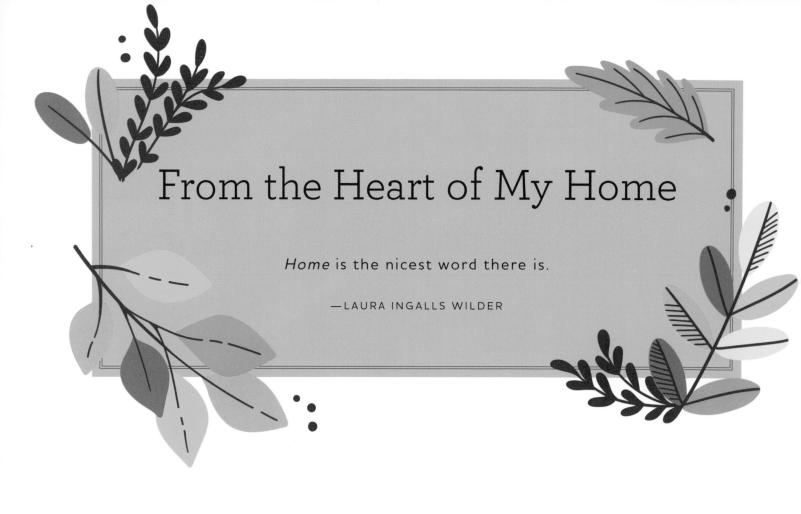

From the Heart of My Home

Home is the nicest word there is.

—LAURA INGALLS WILDER

Family traditions can help us celebrate and feel like we belong. Here are a few family traditions that I hope you follow.

_____

_____

_____

_____

_____

_____

_____

_____

_____

The holiday traditions dear to our hearts each year are _____

_____

_____

_____

_____

_____

_____

_____

_____

_____

_____

_____

_____

_____

_____

_____

_____

_____

Here are some of the best family recipes, straight from your grandfather's table.

_____

_____

Ingredients

_____   _____

_____   _____

_____   _____

_____   _____

_____   _____

_____   _____

Instructions _____

_____

_____

_____

_____

_____

_____

Some of our family's favorite holiday dishes _____

_____

_____

Ingredients

_____   _____

_____   _____

_____   _____

_____   _____

_____   _____

_____   _____

_____   _____

Instructions _____

_____

_____

_____

_____

_____

_____

_____

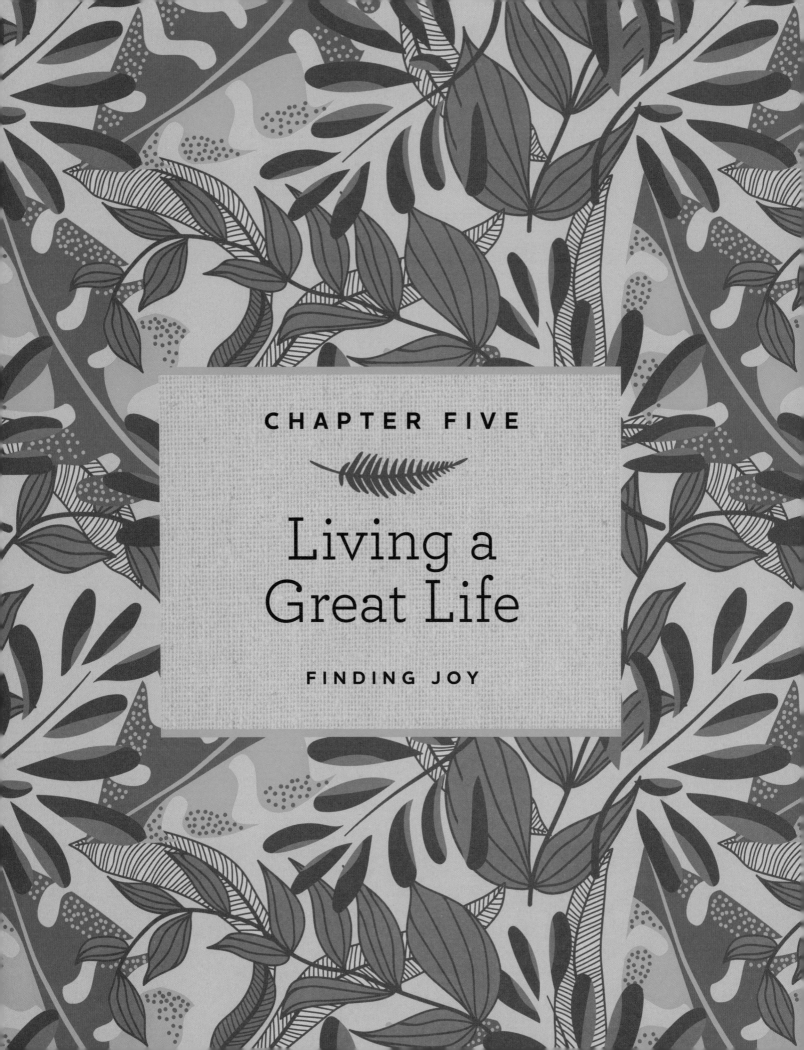

CHAPTER FIVE

Living a Great Life

FINDING JOY

Finding Happy

Happiness is not something ready made.

It comes from your own actions.

—DALAI LAMA

The books that have made me smile are _____

_____

_____

_____

_____

Some of my favorite movies are _____

_____

_____

_____

_____

A sport I love to play or watch is _____

_____

_____

The music that brings me happiness is _____

_____

_____

_____

My favorite song of all is _____

_____

_____

My advice for finding art and music you love is _____

_____

_____

_____

_____

_____

_____

_____

_____

Something I love to do is _____

_____

_____

_____

_____

_____

_____

I am never happier than when I am _____

_____

_____

_____

_____

_____

This is my perfect day _____

_____

_____

_____

_____

72

I share my happy times with you when we _____

_____

_____

_____

_____

_____

My advice for creating happy moments is _____

_____

_____

_____

_____

_____

_____

_____

_____

_____

_____

73

Do What You Love

Happiness is never a step away, it is within you.
You just need to unleash it.

—OJINGIRI HANNAH

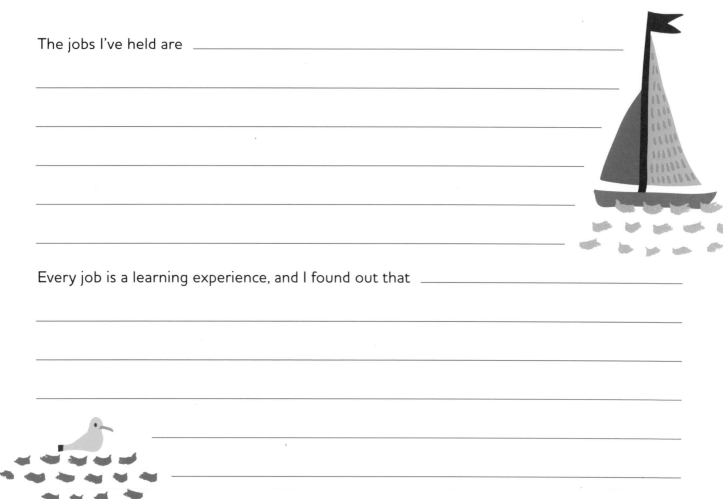

The jobs I've held are _____

_____

_____

_____

_____

Every job is a learning experience, and I found out that _____

_____

_____

_____

_____

One job I will never forget was _____

_____

_____

_____

_____

My advice to you for choosing a career is _____

_____

_____

_____

_____

_____

_____

_____

_____

Always remember this about work _____

_____

_____

_____

_____

_____

_____

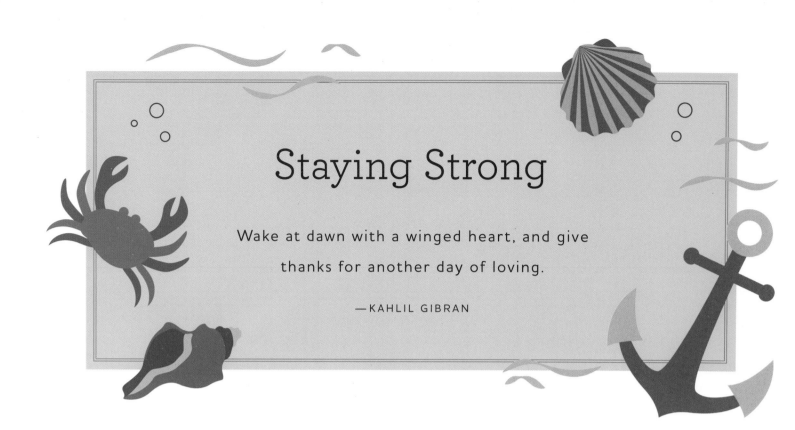

Staying Strong

Wake at dawn with a winged heart, and give thanks for another day of loving.

—KAHLIL GIBRAN

Life is full of ups and downs. But one thing is for sure _____

_____

_____

_____

I know this because _____

_____

_____

_____

_____

_____

_____

When life puts you to the test, remember _____

_____

_____

_____

_____

_____

_____

_____

_____

_____

In troubled times, picture me saying this to you _____

_____

_____

_____

_____

_____

_____

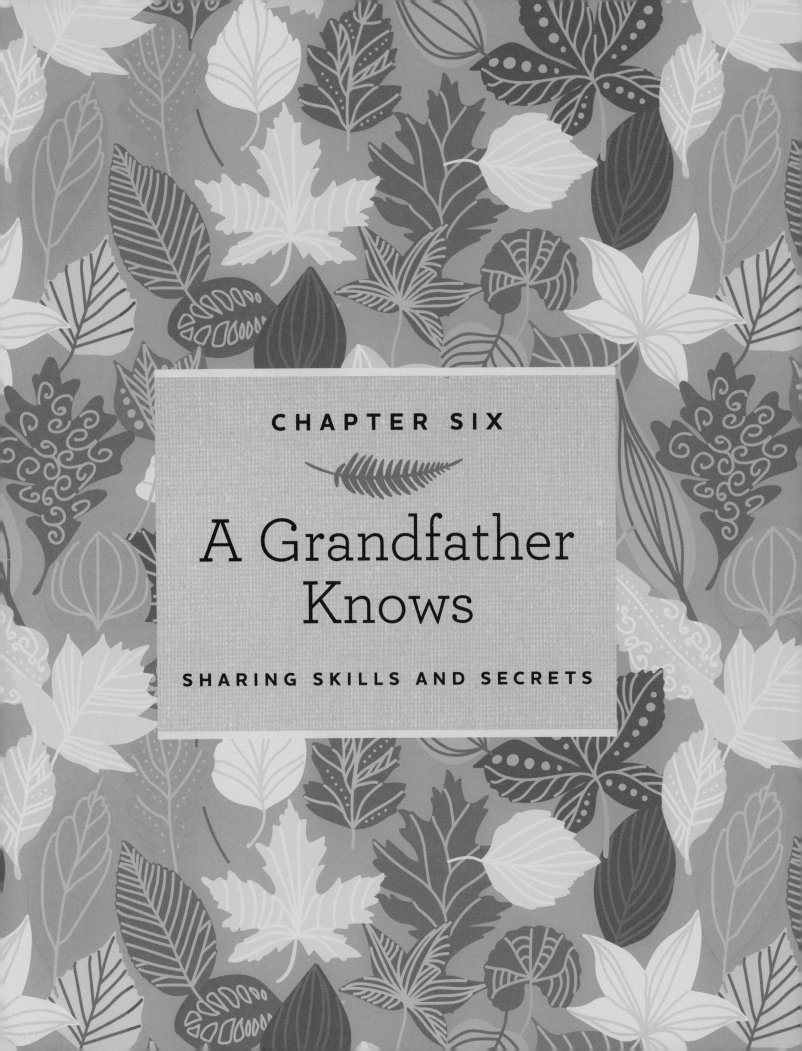

CHAPTER SIX

A Grandfather Knows

SHARING SKILLS AND SECRETS

Be Grateful

We must find time to stop and thank the people
who make a difference in our lives.

—JOHN F. KENNEDY

Take time to count your blessings, because _____

_____

_____

_____

_____

_____

Don't forget the little things like _____

_____

_____

_____

_____

One memorable time someone shared their thanks with me was

_____

_____

_____

I'm grateful to you because _____

_____

_____

_____

This is the way I show it _____

_____

_____

_____

When I look back on my life so far, I feel gratitude for _____

_____

_____

_____

_____

_____

Be Curious

Look up at the stars and not down at your feet.
Try to make sense of what you see, and wonder
about what makes the universe exist. Be curious.

—STEPHEN HAWKING

It's important to stay curious throughout your life because _____

_____

_____

_____

_____

_____

Someone who nurtured my curiosity was _____

_____

_____

_____

_____

When you were little, you were always curious about _____

_____

_____

_____

_____

_____

Here's something I'm curious about _____

_____

_____

_____

_____

_____

_____

I find the best way to get answers is _____

_____

_____

_____

_____

_____

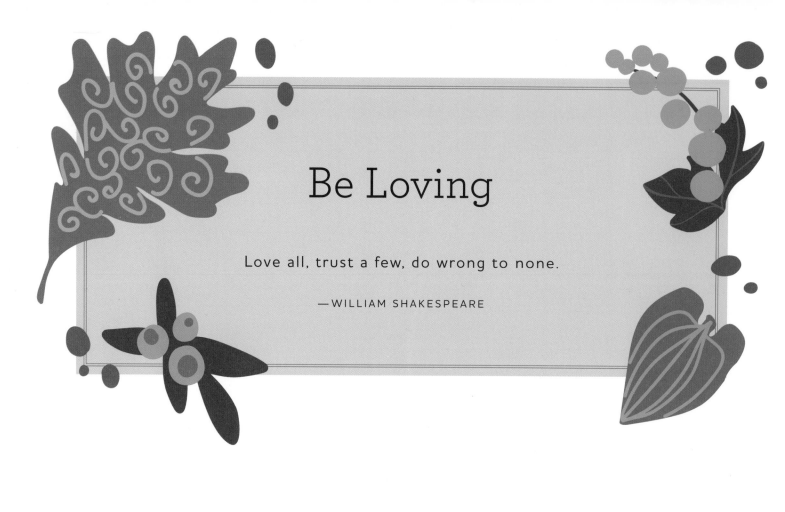

Be Loving

Love all, trust a few, do wrong to none.

—WILLIAM SHAKESPEARE

Love is all you need because _____

_____

_____

_____

_____

_____

Sometimes love isn't easy. For example, _____

_____

_____

_____

_____

This is why being a loving person is so important

_____

_____

_____

_____

_____

These are the ways I've watched you show your love _____

_____

_____

_____

_____

_____

_____

Some ways I like to show my love are _____

_____

_____

_____

_____

_____

Be Positive

You can, you should, and if you're brave enough to start, you will.

—STEPHEN KING

It is worthwhile to stay positive because _____

_____

_____

_____

_____

One time a positive attitude helped me was when _____

_____

_____

_____

_____

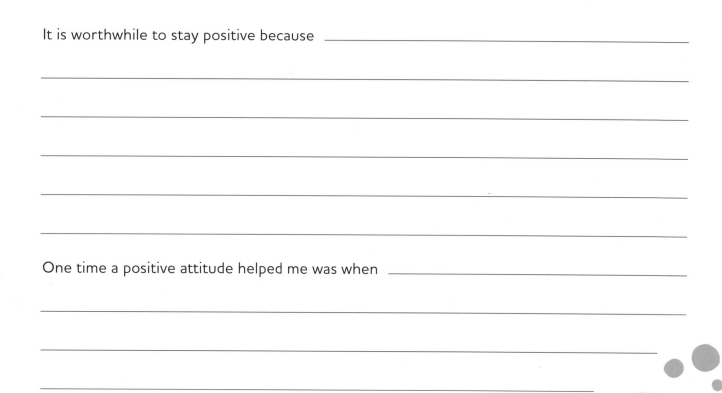

Here's an example of your own positive-thinking power

_____

_____

_____

_____

When I feel down, this is what I think to myself to feel better _____

_____

_____

_____

_____

This story always makes me laugh _____

_____

_____

_____

_____

_____

If life gives you lemons, you can make lemonade, or _____

_____

_____

_____

_____

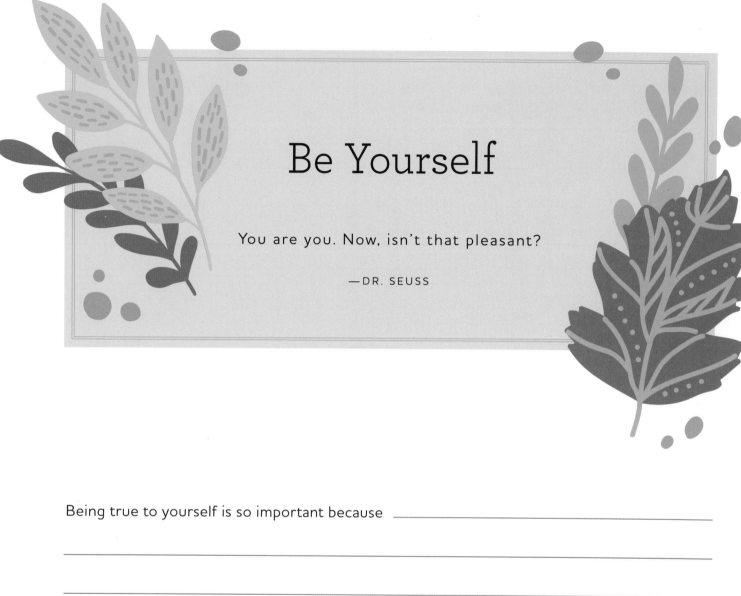

Be Yourself

You are you. Now, isn't that pleasant?

—DR. SEUSS

Being true to yourself is so important because _____

_____

_____

_____

_____

When I had my doubts about being myself, I thought _____

_____

_____

_____

_____

_____

I learned to believe in myself by _____

_____

_____

_____

_____

_____

Something unique about me that I may have passed down to you is _____

_____

_____

_____

_____

_____

_____

Some ways you can make the most of yourself are _____

_____

_____

_____

_____

_____

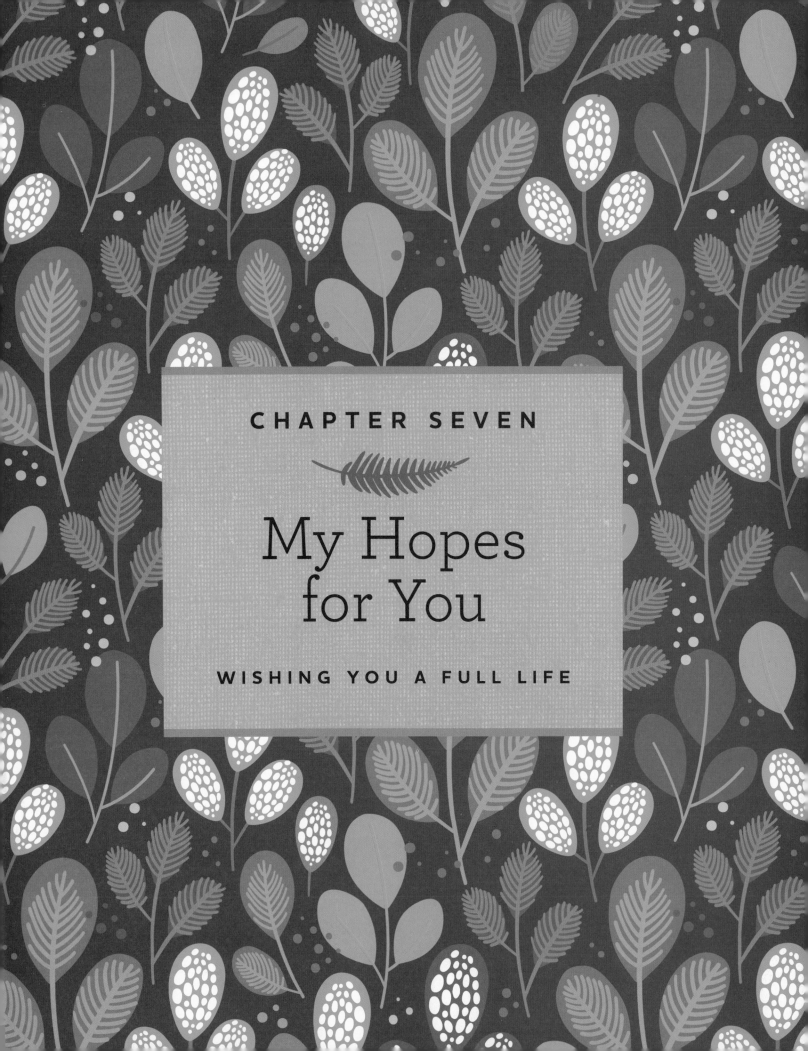

CHAPTER SEVEN

My Hopes for You

WISHING YOU A FULL LIFE

Hello, You

Great fathers get promoted to grandfathers.

—UNKNOWN

How we met for the first time _____

_____

_____

_____

_____

_____

You've found your place in the family as _____

_____

_____

_____

_____

_____

_____

One thing I think you have learned from your family is _____

_____

_____

_____

_____

_____

What I hope you have learned from me is _____

_____

_____

_____

_____

_____

_____

If I could make three wishes come true for you, they would be _____

_____

_____

_____

_____

_____

My Dreams for You

Never forget that you are one of a kind. Never forget that
if there weren't any need for you in all your uniqueness
to be on this Earth, you wouldn't be here at all.

—R. BUCKMINSTER FULLER

I think you are one of a kind because _____

_____

_____

_____

_____

My advice for staying the wonderful person you are is _____

_____

_____

_____

_____

I have so many dreams for you, including _____

_____

_____

_____

_____

_____

_____

You can realize your dreams by _____

_____

_____

_____

_____

_____

_____

_____

I don't know everything, but these are some things I want you to know _____

_____

_____

_____

_____

_____

_____

Message to You

My story in this book is finished, but yours is just beginning. Here is a message from me to you, with all my love and wisdom.

_____

_____

_____

_____

_____

_____

_____

_____

_____

_____